50 Grilled Cheese Recipes to Savor

By: Kelly Johnson

Table of Contents

- Classic American Grilled Cheese
- Bacon and Tomato Grilled Cheese
- Caprese Grilled Cheese
- Mac and Cheese Grilled Cheese
- Avocado and Egg Grilled Cheese
- BBQ Pulled Pork Grilled Cheese
- Turkey and Cranberry Grilled Cheese
- Spicy Jalapeño Grilled Cheese
- Pesto and Mozzarella Grilled Cheese
- Grilled Cheese with Caramelized Onions
- Ham and Swiss Grilled Cheese
- Brie and Pear Grilled Cheese
- Mediterranean Grilled Cheese with Feta and Olive Tapenade
- Buffalo Chicken Grilled Cheese
- Spinach and Artichoke Grilled Cheese
- Roasted Vegetable Grilled Cheese
- Cheese and Mushroom Grilled Cheese
- Philly Cheesesteak Grilled Cheese
- Smoked Gouda and Apple Grilled Cheese
- Bacon, Egg, and Cheese Grilled Cheese
- Lobster and Havarti Grilled Cheese
- Chicken Caesar Grilled Cheese
- Blue Cheese and Walnut Grilled Cheese
- Grilled Cheese with Sun-Dried Tomatoes
- Grilled Cheese with Roasted Garlic
- Eggplant Parmesan Grilled Cheese
- Sweet and Spicy Grilled Cheese with Honey and Sriracha
- Cheddar and Chutney Grilled Cheese
- Truffle and Gruyère Grilled Cheese
- BBQ Chicken Grilled Cheese
- Grilled Cheese with Smoked Salmon
- Jalapeño Popper Grilled Cheese
- Grilled Cheese with Balsamic Glaze and Arugula
- Sweet Potato and Goat Cheese Grilled Cheese
- Grilled Cheese with Sauteed Mushrooms and Swiss

- Cheddar and Pickle Grilled Cheese
- Grilled Cheese with Bacon Jam
- Roasted Red Pepper and Hummus Grilled Cheese
- Tuna Melt Grilled Cheese
- Grilled Cheese with Kimchi
- Grilled Cheese with Eggplant and Mozzarella
- Pastrami and Swiss Grilled Cheese
- Roasted Beet and Goat Cheese Grilled Cheese
- Grilled Cheese with Sautéed Spinach and Ricotta
- French Onion Soup Grilled Cheese
- Grilled Cheese with Avocado and Bacon
- Muenster and Apple Grilled Cheese
- Grilled Cheese with Sweet Chilli Sauce and Chicken
- Grilled Cheese with Zesty Pickled Jalapeños
- Tofu and Vegan Cheese Grilled Cheese

Classic American Grilled Cheese

Ingredients:

- 2 slices of white or whole wheat bread
- 2 tablespoons butter
- 2 slices American cheese

Instructions:

1. Butter one side of each slice of bread.
2. Place a slice of cheese between the unbuttered sides of the bread.
3. Heat a skillet over medium heat and place the sandwich in the pan, buttered side down.
4. Cook for 2-3 minutes on each side, or until golden brown and the cheese has melted.
5. Serve hot!

Bacon and Tomato Grilled Cheese

Ingredients:

- 2 slices of bread
- 2 tablespoons butter
- 2 slices cheddar cheese
- 2 slices cooked bacon
- 2 slices tomato

Instructions:

1. Butter one side of each slice of bread.
2. Place the cheddar cheese, bacon, and tomato slices between the unbuttered sides of the bread.
3. Heat a skillet over medium heat and cook the sandwich for 2-3 minutes per side, until golden brown and the cheese is melted.
4. Serve immediately.

Caprese Grilled Cheese

Ingredients:

- 2 slices of sourdough bread
- 2 tablespoons butter
- 2 slices mozzarella cheese
- 1 small tomato, sliced
- Fresh basil leaves
- Balsamic glaze (optional)

Instructions:

1. Butter the outside of each slice of bread.
2. Layer the mozzarella cheese, tomato slices, and fresh basil between the slices of bread.
3. Grill on medium heat for 2-3 minutes per side until the bread is golden and the cheese is melted.
4. Drizzle with balsamic glaze before serving, if desired.

Mac and Cheese Grilled Cheese

Ingredients:

- 2 slices of bread
- 2 tablespoons butter
- 2 slices cheddar cheese
- 1/2 cup homemade or store-bought macaroni and cheese

Instructions:

1. Butter one side of each slice of bread.
2. Layer a slice of cheddar cheese on each slice of bread.
3. Spoon a generous amount of mac and cheese on top of one slice, then close with the other slice of bread.
4. Grill the sandwich on medium heat for 2-3 minutes per side until the bread is golden brown and the cheese is melted.

Avocado and Egg Grilled Cheese

Ingredients:

- 2 slices of bread
- 2 tablespoons butter
- 1 slice cheddar cheese
- 1/2 avocado, sliced
- 1 egg, scrambled or fried

Instructions:

1. Butter one side of each slice of bread.
2. Cook the egg to your liking (scrambled or fried).
3. Layer the cheddar cheese, avocado slices, and cooked egg between the slices of bread.
4. Grill on medium heat for 2-3 minutes per side, until golden brown and the cheese has melted.

BBQ Pulled Pork Grilled Cheese

Ingredients:

- 2 slices of bread
- 2 tablespoons butter
- 2 slices cheddar cheese
- 1/2 cup pulled pork
- 2 tablespoons barbecue sauce

Instructions:

1. Butter one side of each slice of bread.
2. Layer the cheddar cheese, pulled pork, and a drizzle of barbecue sauce between the slices of bread.
3. Grill the sandwich on medium heat for 2-3 minutes per side until golden brown and the cheese has melted.
4. Serve hot!

Turkey and Cranberry Grilled Cheese

Ingredients:

- 2 slices of bread
- 2 tablespoons butter
- 2 slices Swiss cheese
- 2 slices cooked turkey
- 2 tablespoons cranberry sauce

Instructions:

1. Butter one side of each slice of bread.
2. Layer the Swiss cheese, turkey slices, and cranberry sauce between the slices of bread.
3. Grill on medium heat for 2-3 minutes per side until golden brown and the cheese is melted.
4. Serve immediately!

Spicy Jalapeño Grilled Cheese

Ingredients:

- 2 slices of bread
- 2 tablespoons butter
- 2 slices pepper jack cheese
- 2-3 slices fresh jalapeño
- 1 tablespoon pickled jalapeños (optional)

Instructions:

1. Butter one side of each slice of bread.
2. Place pepper jack cheese and fresh or pickled jalapeño slices between the unbuttered sides of the bread.
3. Grill on medium heat for 2-3 minutes per side until golden brown and the cheese has melted.
4. Serve hot with an extra kick of heat!

Pesto and Mozzarella Grilled Cheese

Ingredients:

- 2 slices of bread
- 2 tablespoons butter
- 2 slices mozzarella cheese
- 2 tablespoons pesto sauce

Instructions:

1. Butter one side of each slice of bread.
2. Spread pesto on the unbuttered sides of the bread, then add mozzarella cheese.
3. Grill on medium heat for 2-3 minutes per side until golden brown and the cheese has melted.
4. Serve with a burst of fresh basil flavor!

Grilled Cheese with Caramelized Onions

Ingredients:

- 2 slices of bread
- 2 tablespoons butter
- 2 slices Gruyère cheese
- 1 large onion, thinly sliced
- 1 tablespoon olive oil
- Salt and pepper to taste

Instructions:

1. In a pan, heat olive oil over medium heat. Add onions, salt, and pepper, cooking for 15-20 minutes, stirring occasionally, until caramelized.
2. Butter one side of each slice of bread.
3. Layer the Gruyère cheese and caramelized onions between the slices of bread.
4. Grill on medium heat for 2-3 minutes per side until golden brown and the cheese is melted.
5. Serve hot!

Ham and Swiss Grilled Cheese

Ingredients:

- 2 slices of bread
- 2 tablespoons butter
- 2 slices Swiss cheese
- 2 slices deli ham

Instructions:

1. Butter one side of each slice of bread.
2. Layer Swiss cheese and ham between the unbuttered sides of the bread.
3. Grill on medium heat for 2-3 minutes per side, until the bread is golden brown and the cheese has melted.
4. Serve immediately!

Brie and Pear Grilled Cheese

Ingredients:

- 2 slices of sourdough bread
- 2 tablespoons butter
- 2-3 slices Brie cheese
- 1 pear, thinly sliced
- Honey (optional)

Instructions:

1. Butter one side of each slice of bread.
2. Place Brie cheese and pear slices between the unbuttered sides of the bread.
3. Grill on medium heat for 2-3 minutes per side until golden brown and the cheese is melted.
4. Drizzle with honey before serving, if desired.

Mediterranean Grilled Cheese with Feta and Olive Tapenade

Ingredients:

- 2 slices of bread
- 2 tablespoons butter
- 2 slices mozzarella cheese
- 2 tablespoons feta cheese, crumbled
- 2 tablespoons olive tapenade

Instructions:

1. Butter one side of each slice of bread.
2. Spread olive tapenade on one slice of bread, then layer mozzarella cheese and feta cheese on top.
3. Grill on medium heat for 2-3 minutes per side until golden brown and the cheese is melted.
4. Serve with a Mediterranean twist!

Buffalo Chicken Grilled Cheese

Ingredients:

- 2 slices of bread
- 2 tablespoons butter
- 2 slices cheddar cheese
- 1/2 cup cooked chicken, shredded
- 2 tablespoons buffalo sauce

Instructions:

1. Butter one side of each slice of bread.
2. Mix the shredded chicken with buffalo sauce and layer it between the slices of bread, along with cheddar cheese.
3. Grill on medium heat for 2-3 minutes per side until golden brown and the cheese is melted.
4. Serve hot for a spicy, savory sandwich!

Spinach and Artichoke Grilled Cheese

Ingredients:

- 2 slices of bread
- 2 tablespoons butter
- 2 slices mozzarella cheese
- 1/4 cup cooked spinach, drained
- 1/4 cup canned artichoke hearts, chopped
- 1 tablespoon cream cheese

Instructions:

1. Butter one side of each slice of bread.
2. Mix the spinach, artichokes, and cream cheese, then spread on one slice of bread.
3. Layer mozzarella cheese on top, and close the sandwich with the other slice of bread.
4. Grill on medium heat for 2-3 minutes per side until golden brown and the cheese is melted.

Roasted Vegetable Grilled Cheese

Ingredients:

- 2 slices of bread
- 2 tablespoons butter
- 2 slices provolone cheese
- 1/2 cup roasted vegetables (such as zucchini, bell peppers, and eggplant)

Instructions:

1. Butter one side of each slice of bread.
2. Layer the roasted vegetables and provolone cheese between the slices of bread.
3. Grill on medium heat for 2-3 minutes per side until golden brown and the cheese is melted.
4. Serve hot for a hearty, veggie-packed grilled cheese.

Cheese and Mushroom Grilled Cheese

Ingredients:

- 2 slices of bread
- 2 tablespoons butter
- 2 slices Swiss cheese
- 1/2 cup sautéed mushrooms
- 1 teaspoon fresh thyme (optional)

Instructions:

1. Butter one side of each slice of bread.
2. Layer the Swiss cheese and sautéed mushrooms (and thyme, if using) between the slices of bread.
3. Grill on medium heat for 2-3 minutes per side until golden brown and the cheese is melted.
4. Serve hot with the earthy flavor of mushrooms.

Philly Cheesesteak Grilled Cheese

Ingredients:

- 2 slices of bread
- 2 tablespoons butter
- 2 slices provolone cheese
- 1/2 cup cooked beef (thinly sliced or shredded)
- 1/4 cup sautéed onions and bell peppers

Instructions:

1. Butter one side of each slice of bread.
2. Layer provolone cheese, cooked beef, and sautéed onions and peppers between the slices of bread.
3. Grill on medium heat for 2-3 minutes per side until golden brown and the cheese is melted.
4. Serve immediately for a classic Philly cheesesteak twist.

Smoked Gouda and Apple Grilled Cheese

Ingredients:

- 2 slices of sourdough bread
- 2 tablespoons butter
- 2 slices smoked Gouda cheese
- 1 small apple, thinly sliced
- 1 teaspoon honey (optional)

Instructions:

1. Butter one side of each slice of bread.
2. Layer smoked Gouda cheese and apple slices between the unbuttered sides of the bread.
3. Drizzle a little honey on top of the apples, if desired.
4. Grill on medium heat for 2-3 minutes per side until golden brown and the cheese is melted.
5. Serve with a sweet and smoky twist!

Bacon, Egg, and Cheese Grilled Cheese

Ingredients:

- 2 slices of bread
- 2 tablespoons butter
- 2 slices cheddar cheese
- 2 slices cooked bacon
- 1 scrambled egg

Instructions:

1. Butter one side of each slice of bread.
2. Layer the cheddar cheese, scrambled egg, and cooked bacon between the slices of bread.
3. Grill on medium heat for 2-3 minutes per side until golden brown and the cheese is melted.
4. Serve hot for a hearty, breakfast-inspired sandwich!

Lobster and Havarti Grilled Cheese

Ingredients:

- 2 slices of bread
- 2 tablespoons butter
- 2 slices Havarti cheese
- 1/2 cup cooked lobster meat, chopped
- 1 tablespoon mayonnaise

Instructions:

1. Butter one side of each slice of bread.
2. Mix the lobster meat with mayonnaise and layer it with Havarti cheese between the slices of bread.
3. Grill on medium heat for 2-3 minutes per side until golden brown and the cheese is melted.
4. Serve with a touch of luxury in every bite!

Chicken Caesar Grilled Cheese

Ingredients:

- 2 slices of bread
- 2 tablespoons butter
- 2 slices mozzarella cheese
- 1/2 cup cooked chicken, shredded
- 1 tablespoon Caesar dressing
- 1 tablespoon grated Parmesan cheese

Instructions:

1. Butter one side of each slice of bread.
2. Mix the shredded chicken with Caesar dressing and layer it with mozzarella and Parmesan cheese between the slices of bread.
3. Grill on medium heat for 2-3 minutes per side until golden brown and the cheese is melted.
4. Serve with a Caesar-inspired twist!

Blue Cheese and Walnut Grilled Cheese

Ingredients:

- 2 slices of bread
- 2 tablespoons butter
- 2 slices of sharp cheddar cheese
- 1/4 cup crumbled blue cheese
- 1/4 cup chopped walnuts

Instructions:

1. Butter one side of each slice of bread.
2. Layer cheddar cheese, crumbled blue cheese, and chopped walnuts between the slices of bread.
3. Grill on medium heat for 2-3 minutes per side until golden brown and the cheese is melted.
4. Serve for a bold and nutty sandwich experience!

Grilled Cheese with Sun-Dried Tomatoes

Ingredients:

- 2 slices of bread
- 2 tablespoons butter
- 2 slices mozzarella cheese
- 2 tablespoons sun-dried tomatoes, chopped
- Fresh basil leaves (optional)

Instructions:

1. Butter one side of each slice of bread.
2. Layer mozzarella cheese and sun-dried tomatoes between the slices of bread, adding fresh basil leaves for extra flavor if desired.
3. Grill on medium heat for 2-3 minutes per side until golden brown and the cheese is melted.
4. Serve with an Italian-inspired touch!

Grilled Cheese with Roasted Garlic

Ingredients:

- 2 slices of bread
- 2 tablespoons butter
- 2 slices provolone cheese
- 2-3 cloves roasted garlic, mashed

Instructions:

1. Butter one side of each slice of bread.
2. Spread mashed roasted garlic on one slice of bread, and layer provolone cheese between the slices of bread.
3. Grill on medium heat for 2-3 minutes per side until golden brown and the cheese is melted.
4. Serve with the savory richness of roasted garlic!

Eggplant Parmesan Grilled Cheese

Ingredients:

- 2 slices of bread
- 2 tablespoons butter
- 2 slices mozzarella cheese
- 2-3 slices of breaded and fried eggplant
- Marinara sauce (for dipping)

Instructions:

1. Butter one side of each slice of bread.
2. Layer mozzarella cheese and fried eggplant slices between the slices of bread.
3. Grill on medium heat for 2-3 minutes per side until golden brown and the cheese is melted.
4. Serve with marinara sauce for dipping.

Sweet and Spicy Grilled Cheese with Honey and Sriracha

Ingredients:

- 2 slices of bread
- 2 tablespoons butter
- 2 slices cheddar cheese
- 1 tablespoon honey
- 1 tablespoon Sriracha sauce

Instructions:

1. Butter one side of each slice of bread.
2. Mix honey and Sriracha sauce together, then spread on the unbuttered side of the bread.
3. Layer cheddar cheese between the slices of bread.
4. Grill on medium heat for 2-3 minutes per side until golden brown and the cheese is melted.
5. Serve for a sweet and spicy sandwich experience!

Cheddar and Chutney Grilled Cheese

Ingredients:

- 2 slices of bread
- 2 tablespoons butter
- 2 slices sharp cheddar cheese
- 2 tablespoons chutney (mango or apple chutney works great)

Instructions:

1. Butter one side of each slice of bread.
2. Spread chutney on the unbuttered side of one slice of bread.
3. Layer cheddar cheese on top of the chutney and close the sandwich.
4. Grill on medium heat for 2-3 minutes per side until golden brown and the cheese is melted.
5. Serve with a sweet and tangy twist!

Truffle and Gruyère Grilled Cheese

Ingredients:

- 2 slices of bread
- 2 tablespoons butter
- 2 slices Gruyère cheese
- 1 tablespoon truffle oil or truffle butter

Instructions:

1. Butter one side of each slice of bread.
2. Drizzle a small amount of truffle oil or spread truffle butter on the unbuttered sides of the bread.
3. Layer Gruyère cheese between the slices of bread.
4. Grill on medium heat for 2-3 minutes per side until golden brown and the cheese is melted.
5. Indulge in the luxurious and earthy flavors of truffle!

BBQ Chicken Grilled Cheese

Ingredients:

- 2 slices of bread
- 2 tablespoons butter
- 2 slices mozzarella cheese
- 1/2 cup cooked chicken, shredded
- 2 tablespoons BBQ sauce

Instructions:

1. Butter one side of each slice of bread.
2. Mix shredded chicken with BBQ sauce, then layer it with mozzarella cheese between the slices of bread.
3. Grill on medium heat for 2-3 minutes per side until golden brown and the cheese is melted.
4. Serve with a smoky, tangy BBQ twist!

Grilled Cheese with Smoked Salmon

Ingredients:

- 2 slices of bread
- 2 tablespoons butter
- 2 slices cream cheese
- 2-3 slices smoked salmon
- Fresh dill (optional)

Instructions:

1. Butter one side of each slice of bread.
2. Spread cream cheese on the unbuttered sides of the bread.
3. Layer smoked salmon and fresh dill between the slices of bread.
4. Grill on medium heat for 2-3 minutes per side until golden brown and the cheese is softened.
5. Serve with a fresh, seafood-inspired twist!

Jalapeño Popper Grilled Cheese

Ingredients:

- 2 slices of bread
- 2 tablespoons butter
- 2 slices cheddar cheese
- 2-3 jalapeños, sliced and sautéed
- 2 tablespoons cream cheese

Instructions:

1. Butter one side of each slice of bread.
2. Spread cream cheese on the unbuttered side of one slice of bread.
3. Layer cheddar cheese and sautéed jalapeños between the slices of bread.
4. Grill on medium heat for 2-3 minutes per side until golden brown and the cheese is melted.
5. Serve with a spicy, creamy kick!

Grilled Cheese with Balsamic Glaze and Arugula

Ingredients:

- 2 slices of bread
- 2 tablespoons butter
- 2 slices mozzarella cheese
- 1/4 cup fresh arugula
- 1 tablespoon balsamic glaze

Instructions:

1. Butter one side of each slice of bread.
2. Layer mozzarella cheese and fresh arugula between the slices of bread.
3. Drizzle balsamic glaze on the inside of one slice of bread.
4. Grill on medium heat for 2-3 minutes per side until golden brown and the cheese is melted.
5. Serve with a fresh, tangy finish!

Sweet Potato and Goat Cheese Grilled Cheese

Ingredients:

- 2 slices of bread
- 2 tablespoons butter
- 2 slices goat cheese
- 1/4 cup roasted sweet potato, mashed
- Fresh thyme (optional)

Instructions:

1. Butter one side of each slice of bread.
2. Spread mashed roasted sweet potato and goat cheese between the slices of bread.
3. Add fresh thyme for extra flavor if desired.
4. Grill on medium heat for 2-3 minutes per side until golden brown and the cheese is melted.
5. Serve with a sweet and creamy contrast!

Grilled Cheese with Sautéed Mushrooms and Swiss

Ingredients:

- 2 slices of bread
- 2 tablespoons butter
- 2 slices Swiss cheese
- 1/2 cup sautéed mushrooms (button or cremini)
- Fresh parsley (optional)

Instructions:

1. Butter one side of each slice of bread.
2. Layer Swiss cheese and sautéed mushrooms between the slices of bread.
3. Sprinkle fresh parsley for added flavor if desired.
4. Grill on medium heat for 2-3 minutes per side until golden brown and the cheese is melted.
5. Serve with earthy, savory goodness!

Cheddar and Pickle Grilled Cheese

Ingredients:

- 2 slices of bread
- 2 tablespoons butter
- 2 slices cheddar cheese
- 3-4 pickle slices (dill or bread-and-butter pickles)

Instructions:

1. Butter one side of each slice of bread.
2. Layer cheddar cheese and pickle slices between the slices of bread.
3. Grill on medium heat for 2-3 minutes per side until golden brown and the cheese is melted.
4. Serve with a tangy crunch!

Grilled Cheese with Bacon Jam

Ingredients:

- 2 slices of bread
- 2 tablespoons butter
- 2 slices sharp cheddar cheese
- 2 tablespoons bacon jam

Instructions:

1. Butter one side of each slice of bread.
2. Spread bacon jam on the unbuttered side of one slice of bread.
3. Layer sharp cheddar cheese on top of the bacon jam and close the sandwich.
4. Grill on medium heat for 2-3 minutes per side until golden brown and the cheese is melted.
5. Enjoy the sweet, savory, and smoky bacon jam paired with the melty cheese!

Roasted Red Pepper and Hummus Grilled Cheese

Ingredients:

- 2 slices of bread
- 2 tablespoons butter
- 2 slices provolone or mozzarella cheese
- 2-3 roasted red pepper slices
- 2 tablespoons hummus

Instructions:

1. Butter one side of each slice of bread.
2. Spread hummus on the unbuttered side of one slice of bread.
3. Layer roasted red pepper slices and cheese between the slices of bread.
4. Grill on medium heat for 2-3 minutes per side until golden brown and the cheese is melted.
5. Savor the creamy hummus and smoky roasted peppers with melted cheese!

Tuna Melt Grilled Cheese

Ingredients:

- 2 slices of bread
- 2 tablespoons butter
- 2 slices Swiss or cheddar cheese
- 1/2 cup tuna salad (tuna, mayo, celery, onion, salt, and pepper)

Instructions:

1. Butter one side of each slice of bread.
2. Spread tuna salad on the unbuttered side of one slice of bread.
3. Layer Swiss or cheddar cheese on top of the tuna salad and close the sandwich.
4. Grill on medium heat for 2-3 minutes per side until golden brown and the cheese is melted.
5. Enjoy the classic tuna melt with a crispy, cheesy finish!

Grilled Cheese with Kimchi

Ingredients:

- 2 slices of bread
- 2 tablespoons butter
- 2 slices cheddar or gouda cheese
- 2 tablespoons kimchi (drained and chopped)

Instructions:

1. Butter one side of each slice of bread.
2. Layer cheese and chopped kimchi between the slices of bread.
3. Grill on medium heat for 2-3 minutes per side until golden brown and the cheese is melted.
4. Serve with a spicy and tangy kimchi twist!

Grilled Cheese with Eggplant and Mozzarella

Ingredients:

- 2 slices of bread
- 2 tablespoons butter
- 2 slices mozzarella cheese
- 2-3 slices roasted eggplant
- Fresh basil (optional)

Instructions:

1. Butter one side of each slice of bread.
2. Layer roasted eggplant, mozzarella cheese, and fresh basil between the slices of bread.
3. Grill on medium heat for 2-3 minutes per side until golden brown and the cheese is melted.
4. Savor the creamy mozzarella and roasted eggplant for a delicious veggie-packed sandwich!

Pastrami and Swiss Grilled Cheese

Ingredients:

- 2 slices of bread
- 2 tablespoons butter
- 2 slices Swiss cheese
- 3-4 slices pastrami
- 1 tablespoon Dijon mustard (optional)

Instructions:

1. Butter one side of each slice of bread.
2. Layer pastrami, Swiss cheese, and a smear of Dijon mustard between the slices of bread.
3. Grill on medium heat for 2-3 minutes per side until golden brown and the cheese is melted.
4. Enjoy a classic deli-inspired grilled cheese!

Roasted Beet and Goat Cheese Grilled Cheese

Ingredients:

- 2 slices of bread
- 2 tablespoons butter
- 2 slices goat cheese
- 2-3 slices roasted beetroot
- Fresh arugula (optional)

Instructions:

1. Butter one side of each slice of bread.
2. Layer roasted beet slices, goat cheese, and arugula between the slices of bread.
3. Grill on medium heat for 2-3 minutes per side until golden brown and the cheese is melted.
4. Relish the earthy beets paired with tangy goat cheese!

Grilled Cheese with Sautéed Spinach and Ricotta

Ingredients:

- 2 slices of bread
- 2 tablespoons butter
- 2 slices mozzarella cheese
- 1/4 cup ricotta cheese
- 1/2 cup sautéed spinach (drained)

Instructions:

1. Butter one side of each slice of bread.
2. Spread ricotta cheese on the unbuttered side of one slice of bread.
3. Add sautéed spinach and mozzarella cheese on top, then close the sandwich.
4. Grill on medium heat for 2-3 minutes per side until golden brown and the cheese is melted.
5. Enjoy the creamy ricotta and fresh spinach in every bite!

French Onion Soup Grilled Cheese

Ingredients:

- 2 slices of bread
- 2 tablespoons butter
- 2 slices Gruyère cheese
- 1/2 cup caramelized onions
- 1 teaspoon beef or vegetable broth concentrate (optional)

Instructions:

1. Butter one side of each slice of bread.
2. Spread a thin layer of broth concentrate on the unbuttered side for extra flavor.
3. Add caramelized onions and Gruyère cheese, then close the sandwich.
4. Grill on medium heat for 2-3 minutes per side until golden brown and the cheese is melted.
5. Relish the rich, savory flavors reminiscent of classic French onion soup!

Grilled Cheese with Avocado and Bacon

Ingredients:

- 2 slices of bread
- 2 tablespoons butter
- 2 slices cheddar cheese
- 2 slices cooked bacon
- 1/2 avocado, sliced

Instructions:

1. Butter one side of each slice of bread.
2. Layer avocado slices, cooked bacon, and cheddar cheese between the slices of bread.
3. Grill on medium heat for 2-3 minutes per side until golden brown and the cheese is melted.
4. Enjoy the creamy avocado paired with crispy bacon and melted cheese!

Muenster and Apple Grilled Cheese

Ingredients:

- 2 slices of bread
- 2 tablespoons butter
- 2 slices Muenster cheese
- 1/2 apple, thinly sliced
- 1 teaspoon honey (optional)

Instructions:

1. Butter one side of each slice of bread.
2. Layer Muenster cheese and apple slices between the slices of bread.
3. Drizzle honey over the apple slices for added sweetness, if desired.
4. Grill on medium heat for 2-3 minutes per side until golden brown and the cheese is melted.
5. Savor the sweet and savory combination of crisp apples and creamy cheese!

Grilled Cheese with Sweet Chili Sauce and Chicken

Ingredients:

- 2 slices of bread
- 2 tablespoons butter
- 2 slices mozzarella or provolone cheese
- 1/4 cup cooked shredded chicken
- 1 tablespoon sweet chili sauce

Instructions:

1. Butter one side of each slice of bread.
2. Toss shredded chicken with sweet chili sauce.
3. Layer sauced chicken and cheese between the slices of bread.
4. Grill on medium heat for 2-3 minutes per side until golden brown and the cheese is melted.
5. Indulge in the sweet, tangy, and slightly spicy flavors of this unique sandwich!

Grilled Cheese with Zesty Pickled Jalapeños

Ingredients:

- 2 slices of bread
- 2 tablespoons butter
- 2 slices pepper jack or cheddar cheese
- 1 tablespoon pickled jalapeño slices

Instructions:

1. Butter one side of each slice of bread.
2. Layer cheese and pickled jalapeños between the slices of bread.
3. Grill on medium heat for 2-3 minutes per side until golden brown and the cheese is melted.
4. Delight in the zesty kick of jalapeños with melty cheese!

Tofu and Vegan Cheese Grilled Cheese

Ingredients:

- 2 slices of bread
- 2 tablespoons vegan butter
- 2 slices vegan cheese
- 1/4 cup marinated tofu, sliced
- Optional: fresh spinach or arugula

Instructions:

1. Butter one side of each slice of bread with vegan butter.
2. Layer marinated tofu, vegan cheese, and optional greens between the slices of bread.
3. Grill on medium heat for 2-3 minutes per side until golden brown and the cheese is melted.
4. Enjoy this plant-based grilled cheese, packed with flavor and texture!

www.ingramcontent.com/pod-product-compliance
Lightning Source LLC
LaVergne TN
LVHW081338060526
838201LV00055B/2722